P9-AFR-497

WELCOME TO THE WORLD OF ANIMALS

Snakes

Diane Swanson

Gareth Stevens Publishing
A WORLD ALMANAC EDUCATION GROUP COMPANY

Please visit our web site at: www.garethstevens.com
For a free color catalog describing Gareth Stevens Publishing's list of high-quality books
and multimedia programs, call 1-800-542-2595 (USA) or 1-800-387-3178 (Canada).
Gareth Stevens Publishing's fax: (414) 332-3567.

The publishers acknowledge the support of the Canada Council for the Arts and the Cultural Services
Branch of the Government of British Columbia in making this publication possible.

Library of Congress Cataloging-in-Publication Data

Swanson, Diane, 1944-
   [Welcome to the world of snakes]
   Snakes / by Diane Swanson. — North American ed.
      p. cm. — (Welcome to the world of animals)
   Includes index.
   Summary: Describes the physical characteristics and behavior of snakes.
   ISBN 0-8368-3318-X (lib. bdg.)
   1. Snakes—Juvenile literature. [1. Snakes.] I. Title.
QL666.O6S89   2002
597.96—dc21   2002021686

This edition first published in 2002 by
Gareth Stevens Publishing
A World Almanac Education Group Company
330 West Olive Street, Suite 100
Milwaukee, WI 53212 USA

This U.S. edition © 2002 by Gareth Stevens, Inc. Original edition © 2001 by Diane Swanson.
First published in 2001 by Whitecap Books, Vancouver. Additional end matter © 2002
by Gareth Stevens, Inc.

Series editor: Patricia Lantier
Design: Katherine A. Goedheer
Cover design: Renee M. Bach

Cover photograph: Kitchin & Hurst/First Light
Photo credits: Wayne Lynch 4, 16, 18, 26, 30; Nate Kley 6; Mark Snyder, Natural Selections/First Light
8; B. Milne/First Light 10; A.B. Sheldon/Dembinsky Photo Assoc. 12; Kenneth Krysko 14; Medford
Taylor/First Light 20; Tim Christie/TimChristie.com 22; Joel Sartore/First Light 24; Natural
Selections/First Light 28

Printed in the United States of America

1 2 3 4 5 6 7 8 9 06 05 04 03 02

Contents

World of Difference 5

Where in the World 9

World of Words 13

World in Motion 17

World of Senses 21

World Full of Food 25

New World 29

Glossary and Index 32

World of Difference

S-s-snakes s-s-simply s-s-slither. Having no legs, they get around just fine on their bellies. Their covering of scaly skin protects them from sharp rocks and rough sand. It keeps them from drying out, too. But a snake's skin is never slimy, as people often think.

Compared to most other animals, snakes have long, slender bodies. Some kinds also have special features. A horned rattlesnake has "horns" that prevent its eyes from getting covered when it buries itself in sand. A hognose snake has a turned-up nose that's useful in burrowing for food.

Like other snakes, this big boa constrictor is covered with tough scales.

No, it's not a worm — it's a tiny thread snake that burrows underground.

Of the 2,500 to 3,000 different kinds of snakes on Earth, about 500 live in North America. Some of the shortest are the skinny thread snakes — only 4½ to 6 inches (11 to 15 centimeters) in length. One of the longest snakes in North America — found in southern Mexico — is the boa constrictor. Although it often grows about 6 feet (2 meters) long, it can reach 16½ feet (5 meters)!

Many snakes are dull colors — brown, gray, and black. Blending in with rocks, sand, and branches, they are less likely to be noticed by their enemies, such as eagles and hawks. The snakes also can sneak up on animals they want to eat. The skin of the boa constrictor, for instance, is a mix of light and dark shades, which helps the snake hide in the flickering sunlight and shadows of the forest.

LEGGY SNAKE

In 2000, an international science team reported rediscovering the remains of a snake in a museum drawer in Jerusalem. About 95 million years ago, the snake had swum the seas off Israel. Its mouth would have opened WIDE — like the mouth of today's boas and pythons, which swallow food much bigger than themselves.

Surprisingly, the ancient snake had legs — back legs too short to help it move. No one knows how they were used, but the answer might lie in another museum drawer!

Where in the World

Snakes show up almost everywhere. They live on every continent in the world, except Antarctica. Most find homes where the climate is warm, but some have adapted to cool weather. The common garter snake, for example, even manages to live in southern parts of Alaska and Canada's Northwest Territories.

Different kinds of snakes settle in different kinds of homes, including damp woods, dry deserts, open grasslands, muggy swamps, and cool streams. Some snakes live right in the water, but most spend the

A rough green snake spends a lot of its time in the trees.

9

bulk of their time on land or in trees. A few burrow underground.

Snakes don't have a lot of fat to help keep their body temperatures steady, and they don't make much heat of their own. Instead, they lie in sunshine to warm up and head for shade — or sometimes bury themselves in sand — to cool down.

Garter snakes take several days to warm up after wintering together in a pit.

Surviving cold winters can be hard for snakes. That's why many of them enter dens, such as burrows and caves, during the fall. Tucked away, they stay warm enough to live, but not to be active. Their breathing and heartbeats slow down, and they sleep deeply — or hibernate — for months.

Where winters are especially cold, only a few dens may be deep enough for snakes to avoid freezing — so they share. In some areas, thousands of common garter snakes gather in the same pit each year.

SNAKE MARVELS

Snakes are surprising! Here are some of the reasons why:

- **An eastern screech-owl may put a thread snake in its nest to eat pests, such as tiny insects.**

- **A snake can keep its mouth closed and stick its tongue out through a notch in its top lip.**

- **For a while, even a DEAD rattlesnake can snap its jaws shut and release poison.**

World of Words

You can hear, see, even smell snakes "talking." During breeding seasons, female snakes release scents — signals that they are ready to mate. Males can follow these scents over long distances. But if snakes are threatened, their smells have quite a different meaning — "Go away." Glands near their back ends ooze a liquid that can stink for several hours.

Most snakes also hi-s-s to communicate. The sound can be enough to stop enemies, such as skunks and foxes, in their tracks. By pretending to strike, snakes can make their message stronger.

Dead — or not? This upside-down hognose snake is probably just pretending.

13

This coral snake's bright bands signal danger, but similar nonpoisonous snakes might fool you.

The poisonous rattlesnake rattles out warnings with its tail. When jiggled, hard rings at the tip of the tail buz-z-z. Whatever is creeping close to the snake had better move away — or else.

Snakes that aren't poisonous sometimes shake their tails, too. If they are nestled among dry leaves or loose stones, they can sound a lot like rattlesnakes. A snake-eating animal might not stick around to discover the difference.

Bright colors on snakes can act as alarms, frightening or startling their enemies. A coral snake, for instance, is covered in bands of red, white, and black that warn, "I'm poisonous." Snakes such as cottonmouths open their mouths wide and display a warning color inside. A ringneck snake can startle another animal by exposing red scales beneath its tail.

PLAYING DEAD

A hognose snake can be a ham. Bother it and the snake coils up, hisses loudly, and spreads out a "hood" of skin. It rarely bites, but it might strike — with its mouth closed. All this is to say, "Back off."

Don't get the message? The hognose releases a strong smell and displays the purple color inside its mouth. Still don't understand? The snake falls on its back — mouth open and tongue hanging out. "Leave me alone," it is saying, "I'm dead anyway."

World in Motion

Snakes crawl, climb, or swim well —
without any legs. Many snakes can move
in all three ways, but some are designed
to do one or another best.

A long spine made of many small bones
called vertebrae helps snakes move. Each
vertebra is connected to a pair of ribs. The
ribs are attached by muscles to large scales
on the snakes' belly. The muscles push and
pull these scales as the animals travel.

Snakes normally crawl by bending their
bodies into S-shaped curves. They wriggle
forward by moving the scales along the
back of each curve and pressing against

Pausing to check
things out, this fast-
moving racer will be
gone in a flash.

17

Sidewinders don't travel forward in the direction they face. Instead, they move sideways.

bumps on the ground. Snakes also swim in this S-shaped way, pushing their bodies against the water.

When snakes climb, their belly scales catch on the rough bark of trees. Some snakes, such as corn snakes, squeeze themselves into splits in the bark and crawl almost straight up. Tree boas can climb even smooth trees by grabbing a branch with their tails, looping their front ends around a higher branch, and pulling themselves up.

Traveling across loose sand calls for a special method of crawling. A sidewinder, such as a horned rattlesnake, lifts the front of its body and throws it sideways. As it lands, the snake flings the back part of its body, then it tosses the front part again — on and on. That way, the snake can move quickly and keep much of its body off the burning sand.

WILD RACERS

Super-slim, super-long snakes called racers earn their name. In the trees or on the ground, they are among the fastest snakes on Earth. As they dart around, hunting for food, racers appear to move like lightning.

A racer's ropelike build creates a false impression, though. Its peak speed is only 4 miles (6 kilometers) an hour — slow for many runners, including you. Still, in the world of snakes, racers are amazingly fast.

World of Senses

No winking. No blinking. Without lids, snakes can't close their eyes, even when they are asleep. But they do have "spectacles." Rounded, see-through scales cover and protect their eyes at all times.

Most snakes see well. Their eyes focus much like cameras do, by moving the lenses forward and backward. These lenses are often yellowish — not clear. The color screens out some of the light rays and makes it easier for snakes to see in bright light. The lenses of racers are among the deepest yellow, helping these snakes spot fast-moving animals, such as frogs and lizards.

Flick. Flick. The tongue of a king snake tests the air for smells.

Don't look for outer ears on a snake. It doesn't have any, but some sound vibrations can reach its inner ears. The snake's body can also feel vibrations in the ground. That's how it senses a hiker's footsteps. Still, when it comes to finding food, all these vibrations don't seem to help a snake much. For that, it depends on its tongue to find tastes and

Pits between the rattlesnake's eyes and nostrils sense heat.

smells in the air or on the ground.

As a snake hunts, it flicks out its long, forked tongue every few seconds to sample the air. Then it sticks the tips of the tongue into two pockets of an organ in the roof of its mouth. The Jacobson's organ analyzes tastes and smells, helping the snake find dinner — or sense enemies or mates. As the snake moves closer to a meal, its tongue might also act as a feeler.

HUNTING BY HEAT

It's great to have pits in your head — if you're a pit viper, such as a rattlesnake, cotton-mouth, or copperhead. Nerves in paired pits on the faces of these vipers detect the temperatures of things — living or not.

Hunting in total darkness, a pit viper can find a mouse hiding under fallen leaves. The snake can sense the difference in warmth between the mouse and the leaves. It can tell exactly where the mouse is and strike with deadly accuracy.

23

World Full of Food

All snakes eat animals — but some are pickier eaters than others. Redbelly snakes, for example, feed mostly on slugs, and thread snakes gobble up a lot of termites. But many snakes, such as garters, gulp down nearly anything they can — from worms and insects to mice and frogs.

Snakes can't chew their food, so most swallow it whole. The food is often bigger around than they are, but snakes are built to handle the job. Their jaws are loosely connected, so they can open WIDE. Their skin stretches, and their ribs spread apart to make room for whatever the snakes take in.

As it strikes, the diamondback rattlesnake bares its fangs.

A cottonmouth
catches a fish for
dinner, swallowing
it head first.

Small animals that can't fight back are
commonly swallowed alive. Others are
first killed or made helpless. Snakes such
as rattlesnakes have long hollow teeth,
called fangs, which are specially built for
injecting poison. These upper teeth
normally lie flat, but they flip forward
instantly as the snakes strike. Poison

stored in the snakes' jaws is injected through the fangs.

Rat snakes, king snakes, boas, and some others kill by squeezing. They usually grab an animal by the front of its body, then coil around it — tighter and tighter. They are not trying to crush the animal, just stop it from breathing. Once that happens, the snakes relax their hold and start swallowing — which can take more than an hour. Depending on the size of the animal and the temperature of the air, digesting the meal can take several days.

LIGHT LUNCH

It sounded like a good plan. Put fake eggs — light bulbs — in chicken nests to encourage hens to lay real eggs there. But a pine snake came along and swallowed two of the fake eggs. Luckily, the chicken owner noticed the bulbs were missing. When she spotted the snake with its two big lumps, she took it for help. The bulbs were removed through surgery, and the snake survived. Eggshells wouldn't have hurt the pine snake, but the glass bulbs would have!

New World

Rotten logs can make great nests for snakes. So can fallen leaves, sandy soil, and compost heaps. Egg-laying snakes — such as racers and hognose snakes — search for places that are warm, damp, and hidden away. There, they may lay one egg or many. A snake rarely produces more than 50 eggs at a time, but one mud snake in Florida was found with 104!

Mud snakes are one of the few types of snakes that guard their eggs until they hatch. Most others leave their eggs soon after laying them. About six to twelve weeks later, little snakes use a special tooth

Hatching from its leathery egg, a hognose snake takes its first peek at the world.

After shedding, a bull snake left behind a layer of scaly skin.

on their upper jaw to break out of the shell. The tooth soon falls off.

Many other snakes, such as rosy boas, garter snakes, and water snakes, don't need nests at all. They keep their eggs inside their bodies, where their young are well protected. The new snakes may be born live — hatched from thin-shelled eggs inside their mothers.

Newly arrived snakes look after themselves. They feed mainly on little animals, including insects. Right from birth, rattlesnakes are equipped with poison and fangs for hunting food such as lizards. Snakes grow fast when they are young and have plenty of food. And they never completely stop growing. Small snakes can live as long as twelve years. Large snakes might live to be more than forty.

OFF WITH THE OLD

As snakes outgrow and wear out their skins, they grow new ones. Then they simply shed the old, outer skins. But the job takes a while. First, a snake produces a fluid that helps separate the old and new layers. Next, it rubs its head against something firm — pushing back the old skin — and gradually wriggles out.

The old skin, now inside out, is left behind. Young snakes usually shed their skins more often than adults do.

Glossary

adapted — changed to fit different conditions, such as weather.

burrow — (v) to dig a hole or tunnel in the ground.

compost — a mixture of decaying leaves and grass used for fertilizing soil.

constrictor — any snake that kills its prey by tightly squeezing it with its body.

digesting — changing food in the stomach and intestines so that it can be used by the body.

glands — parts of the body that produce fluid from materials in the bloodstream.

lenses — the clear, curved parts of the eyes that focus light rays.

ooze — to flow out slowly through small openings.

scales — the thin, hard plates that cover the body of a snake or other reptile.

shedding — molting; casting off and getting rid of something, such as skin.

Index

bellies 5, 17, 18
body temperatures 10, 11
burrowing 5, 6, 10

colors 7, 15, 21
communicating 13-15

dens 11

ears 22
eggs 29, 30
enemies 7, 13, 23

eyes 5, 21

fangs 25, 26, 27, 31
food 5, 7, 19, 22, 25, 31

hibernating 11

Jacobson's organ 23
jaws 11, 25, 30

nests 29, 30

poisons 11, 14, 26, 31

scales 5, 15, 17, 18, 21
shedding 30, 31
skin 5, 7, 15, 25, 30, 31
smelling 13, 15, 21, 23
swallowing 7, 25, 26, 27
swimming 7, 17, 18

tails 14, 15, 19
tasting 22, 23
teeth 26, 29, 30, 31
tongues 11, 15, 21, 22, 23